KV-677-463

WORD OF MOUTH

EDITED BY

Ruth Carr, Gráinne Tobin, Sally Wheeler and Ann Zell

WORD OF MOUTH POETRY COLLECTIVE

Ruth Carr
Margaret Curran
Elaine Gaston
Pia Gore
Ann McKay
Eilish Martin
Joan Newmann
Kate Newmann
Gráinne Tobin
Mary Twomey
Sally Wheeler
Ann Zell

THE
BLACKSTAFF PRESS

BELFAST

30630
(3. 6. 04)

First published in 1996 by
The Blackstaff Press Limited
3 Galway Park, Dundonald, Belfast BT16 0AN, Northern Ireland
with the assistance of
The Arts Council of Northern Ireland

© Word of Mouth Poetry Collective, 1996
Copyright of individual poems remains with individual authors
All rights reserved

Typeset by Techniset Typesetters, Newton-le-Willows, Merseyside

Printed by in England by Cox and Wyman Limited

A CIP catalogue record for this book
is available from the British Library

ISBN 0-85640-584-1

CONTENTS

ACKNOWLEDGEMENTS

Word of Mouth Poetry Collective wishes to thank the Linen Hall Library for its generous provision of meeting facilities, Downtown Women's Centre and *Women's News* for computer facilities, the Arts Council of Northern Ireland and Northern Ireland Voluntary Trust for grants towards the work of the group, and the Tyrone Guthrie Centre, Annaghmakerrig, where the idea for this collection first took shape.

Some of these poems have previously appeared in the *Atlanta Review*, the *Belfast Telegraph*, *Cúirt Journal*, *Gown Literary Supplement*, *HU (Honest Ulsterman)* *Krino*, *Peterloo Poets 6*, *Poetry Ireland Review*, *Stet*, the *Sunday Tribune*'s 'New Irish Writing', *Verse*, *Writing Women* and *Women's Work III* and *VI*, and three poems have been broadcast on BBC Radio Ulster, BBC Radio 2, and on BBC 1 Northern Ireland.

INTRODUCTION

This anthology is a celebration of women's voices. While the poems are the work of Word of Mouth Poetry Collective, they are not collective poems; they are the distinctive work of each individual writer. This is our contribution to the blossoming of poetry from women in the north of Ireland and throughout the world.

Word of Mouth Poetry Collective, like so many writing groups, was born out of a need for contact with other writers. We wanted to create an environment in which our poetry would thrive, uninhibited and uncensored (at least by others if not entirely by self), where it would be taken seriously. Primarily our concern is with poetics – in both a pure and a practical sense. Our preoccupation is with the business of word-craft in ferrying ideas and feelings across the water of silence. Unlike the tiger in Kate Newmann's poem, who chose to drown rather than swim after a life lived in 'Such a small space/That every ugly inch was intimate', we want our poems to swim across the stagnating moat. As Mary Twomey indicates in 'Eoin's haiku', poetry, like every meaningful communication, is a two-way process;

> If you smile I shall
> part the bright wave for you, be
> a lamp to your feet.

Drawing on our previous experience of creative writing groups, we were clear from the start what this group was about and how it would operate. Each of us is writer, reader and facilitator in turn at our sessions, each with an equal say in, and responsibility for, all that the group does. Some travel distances – from Ballycastle, Omagh, Down-patrick, Newcastle – others only a mile or two to meet once a month in the Linen Hall Library in Belfast. We have been doing this for several years now, expressly to appraise and encourage one another's work. You could not pay for the quality of critical attention gained in this process. Essentially we are listening to one another as poets and being heard in a society which has not been known for its receptivity to the work of women in any sphere. We live in a place of passionate history, where women's history goes largely unsung and unrecognised. We cannot afford to forget that our heritage has been a divisive one, in terms of gender as well as religion, politics, class, dis/ability, sexuality and race. It is crucial that voices from all quarters are articulated and heard. And while it has not always been possible or safe for that to be so, poetry in the North – as in many divided and war-torn societies throughout the world – has the imaginative scope to counter silences of very different kinds. For instance, Gráinne Tobin's witty and moving poem, 'Ladies' night', in which

> A dozen women settling round a table,
> in the community centre proudly
> muralled in red-white-and-blue . . .

make a 'rag-rug' poem of their experiences as 'army wives always on duty', trusting and risking the poet, in order to do so:

> we bind with secrecy,
> names, ranks, addresses to be left behind,
> remnants of these salvaged lives,
> when I return to mine, the other, side.

A different silence is broached in Eilish Martin's poem, 'A death in autumn', in which she gives voice to a woman condemned to death by hanging according to the laws of the ancient society in which she lived.

Of course, there are constraints which our meetings cannot dispel, such as lack of time, of opportunity, of publishing and performance outlets, and so on. Rather than complain about this state of affairs, we agreed to become more visible: to run readings and workshops with other writing groups. We even put on a festival in Ballycastle in 1993 – one of a series initiated by poet Noelle Vial in Killybegs, County Donegal, and taken up by a number of other groups, including Belfast and Newtownards writers' groups.

In retrospect, our efforts can be seen as part of a growing movement challenging the traditional, confining categories into which the arts (and writing in particular) have been boxed. The hierarchical distinction between community and academia, amateur and professional, popular and élite, is of dubious value. Serious artists tend not to be taken seriously if they are too closely associated with community writing; part-time writers (often the halfway house which women stop at – for historical, social and personal reasons) do not take themselves seriously, alienated by these distinctions. You cannot help questioning the thinking behind such a dual value system, particularly when you look at how a piece of work may be judged according to which 'side' it is deemed to be coming from rather than by its content. It is only by engaging with the work itself that we can come to trust and develop our own judgement instead of relying on a readymade yardstick which has so often proved to be at best a crude and inaccurate approximation, at worst completely missing the mark. You only have to think of Emily Dickinson for the classic example of someone who was so rebuffed by blinkered criticism that 'in her lifetime [she] saw her name in print only once – when she won second prize for Rye and Indian bread at the Amherst Show' (Donna Dickinson, *Emily Dickinson*, 1985).

Many of the poems in this anthology question given perspectives. Running through Joan Newmann's deceptively pastoral vignettes of Greek women, there is an undercurrent against the tide of orthodoxy. This surfaces in 'Kiria Maria' to challenge religious teaching by effectively overshadowing the Church's pronouncement on disability, 'That child is a judgment of God' – 'That child should not have been born', with the silent, supremely Marian image of Mother and Child. A shared concern with the impact of given perspectives results in very different poems. Ann McKay deftly poeticises the childhood game 'The farmer wants a wife' to mirror complex social dynamics while simultaneously subverting them. In 'Of earth and air', Eilish Martin reclaims the experience of birth in a deeply symbolic poem which creates its own myth by disowning a standard one:

> Though you laboured in a shortened bed between
>   narrow sheets biting on your tongue
> till it bled I was born elsewhere.
>
> My birthing pool can be found in the meltwater of a
>   dream where you
> briefly stood your ground ...

The concept of an anthology of our work seemed like a logical step to extend our readership. Despite the upsurge of women poets in Ireland, comparatively few have been published from the North – and those only in very recent years. The highest ratio of women poets to men to appear in an anthology of Irish poetry since the 1960s is four to seventeen (*The New Younger Irish Poets*, ed. Gerald Dawe, Blackstaff Press, 1991). However, while there is a very generous representation of northerners in this collection, none of them are women. In several anthologies of modern Irish and Northern Irish poetry there are no women at all or, at best, one or two. One of the main reasons for this discrepancy is to do with selection procedures. Editors of anthologies usually select work only from those poets who have already been published in book form. This auto-matically rules out most women poets in the North. However, things are changing. At least four women living in Northern Ireland – plus two from Donegal – brought out début collections in 1995, one of them a member of Word of Mouth, Joan Newmann. There is a growing awareness that women do write poetry and that both men and women read poetry regardless of gender. We hope that this anthology will go some way towards closing the gap, that it will indicate to readers that there are many women out there writing poetry worth reading, and that it will encourage others to close the gap still further.

The poets in this anthology come from both sides of the divide and neither side. All have lived for at least fifteen years in the North, most of them all their lives. Some bring the experience of growing up in another place to their poetry, creating poems out of that experience but also poems which look into cultural aspects of Northern Ireland from the outside. Ann Zell offers poems about her Idaho upbringing and poems about living in Ireland – such as her restrained encounter with a German tourist in 'Interlude' and her witty comments in 'Nature programme' on the particular significance of overhead noise in this part of the world:

> Before there were helicopters
>   there were dragonflies.
> And will be, after.

'Family values' is a term that has been exploited to the hilt by politicians and moralisers over the last decade, when of course the family can be a force for good *or* bad – and is usually a mixture of both. This theme is explored by several poets with subtlety. A child's perspective is the focus in Margaret Curran's 'Heartburn' and Elaine Gaston's 'Punishment', whereas a retrospective viewpoint is ex-pressed in Ann Zell's 'Fossil fuel' and Ruth Carr's 'We share the same skin'. Frequently a fusion of both coincides, as in Kate Newmann's 'My mother and I painting Galway Bay' and Pia Gore's 'Tractor to Glenaan'.

Some of us have come late to writing, some have written all our lives. For some reason it is only deemed appropriate to describe writers as 'emerging' if they are youngish. This seems ageist and certainly ignorant of how women (such as northern novelists Janet McNeil and Frances Molloy) come to writing in fits and starts with many interruptions along the way. As Tillie Olsen has pointed out in her collection of essays, *Silences* (1965):

> Compared to men writers of like distinction and years of life, few women writers have had lives of unbroken productivity, or leave behind a body of work. Early beginnings, then silence . . . clogged late ones . . . long periods between books . . . characterise most of us.

Regardless of our individual ages, we could all be described as emerging poets – emerging from the silence and invisibility of women who have been writing poetry for years, yet only now are getting around to challenging our own and others' tunnel vision about what can claim a place on the bookshelf. We hope you enjoy these poems.

RUTH CARR
BELFAST
MAY 1996

EILISH MARTIN

OF EARTH AND AIR

Though you laboured in a shortened bed between
   narrow sheets biting on your tongue
till it bled I was born elsewhere.

My birthing pool can be found in the meltwater of a
   dream where you
briefly stood your ground,

your skirt caught on the yellow gorse abandoned for a
   loose shift
of water, your feet bedded

on pebbles the colour of pewter, your arms a hoop of
   shadow
nursing my head in its lap.

And you, a curse under your breath, knotting the bright
thread you were already winding
back into your purse,

my upside-down screech, held by the heels, mocking
the howl of the north wind in the gorse
bloating your skirt.

PARADISE FATIGUE

Above the falling blade of the Hatchet Field a cloud
    shrouds, a star
hums, a moon pendulums, a merlin scythes the air
with angled wings, a wind sings in the cat's cradle
of a transmission aerial.

Below Black Mountain a kneeling cherub with a
    fractured wing
swings from the jib of a crank-and-ratchet crane
in a monumental sculptor's yard strewn
with half-engraved memorials.

Under the sign of two beaten angels hanging by a
    brazen wing
at the place where six roads cross
a stolen Zephyr brakes spilling
strings of Angel Dust.

Elsewhere the wings of a broadsheet fold round the
    globe of a hazard
lamp alternating in circuits of blips and quarks
a quirk of light in the spaces
between the words.

FLAW

The door into the street banged behind him
Sending shock waves through the house.

She picked up her knitting and paid out a string of wool
From the coiled skein, reining in the slack
At the knitting end where the clack
Of needles recited the Aran story in gossipy rhythms,
The scheming needles telling a tale,
Idling away the waiting till he returned.

Cable-twists, blackberry-knots, moss-weaves
Spoke about an island race of fishermen
Pitched in currachs
Against switchback breakers,
Hauling fish from generation to generation.
And their women walking the shore,
Tide tugging surf-shackled feet,
Eyes skinned for boats black
Nippling the swell, ripe blobs of bramble fruit,
Praying their incantations might pull them in
On rosary cords before the sea
Would pluck and net them in tangle weed.

A weave of women on moss thirsting
Lips brine-washed, slaked
By the blood-letting of blackberry-
Stained tongues honing over dead men's bones.

She counted out the stitches she knew by rote
Noting the Aran women made a flaw
So that fleshed bones redressed by salt
Could be claimed by his own recognising her fault.

Then he was there, his face as off-white
As the unwashed wool she cradled in her lap
As oily, with the swelt of tears greasing his cheeks

My friend is dead, my friend is dead, my friend is dead

The one phrase repeating and repeating
As if the rhythm made the words less hard to say.

She held him fast for as long as she could
Until there was nothing else for it but to let him go
And watch as he hauled himself to bed.

4711

She wore Eau de Cologne 4711 like a PIN number
discreetly.
In her bottom drawer french knickers and camisoles
picked up her scent while
she slept. Mother-of-pearl buttoned cuffs, detachable
lace collars left
a trace. On the wrist. On the pulse below the ear.
Between finger and thumb
she held its negative, in a gloved hand. Hemlines
rumoured it
in the hollow behind the knee. In the vanity purse
of her handbag
there was an empty bottle, without a stopper.

She taught me to wear all perfume that way;
on a garment's edge, on a tissue
of lingerie, on an empty hanger
at the back of a wardrobe.
L'Aimant, Ecstasie, L'Enfant Perdu, Poison.
Memorised, then folded away.

BRUISED

She wore a bruised strawberry
over her left breast.
I would never have guessed
had I not seen her undress
the summer I shared her bed,
the summer of grandfather's death.
She called it, 'my allotment'.

        Seeing my eyes linger
she explained it was given her
one summer in the plots
by a man who smelt
of mould and old tobacco.
Not that she had wanted more
than a lettuce, the root
intact with soil,
to please her mother

        at home
stitching false hems by hand,
turning collars starting to fray;
and she had the coin to pay
in a purse that hung
about her neck. But he took her
by surprise

        with flowers:
the pink blue-flushed spike of lupin,
the foil of gypsophila's white veil
enticing her in to the mildew
grey of his shed
to show the secret tufted bed
where wild strawberries grow,
and.

When she turned to go
she slipped on some trodden thing,
falling against the nail
that ripped her purse, spilling
its coppers on the earthen floor,
and tore the flesh above her breast,
which healed in its chastened way
to resemble a bruised strawberry
clotting close to her heart.

All that summer I lay
in the heat of her widow's bed
wide-eyed while she slept,
looking at the bruised fruit
she wore pinned to her breast,
unsure of how to say
I would wear it for her
when she was dead.

A DEATH IN AUTUMN

They probably caught her in another man's bed
And it being *Samhain* (the evidence suggests) their
  outrage led
To a ritual retribution. Naturally
There were procedures; that would have been fully
Understood by every party concerned
Including the victim whose role in these affairs was just
  as learned
As that of prosecutor, judge and foreman of the jury.
Although, if truth be told, one actor (masked) usually
  played all three;
And if he felt inclined to extemporise
The mob (in the pit or in the gods) would be none the
  wiser
Believing the script was sealed
By the wand that marked her flesh for the common weal.

They have untied the knots of my apron strings,
Unhooked my bodice, loosed my gathered skirt, pulled off my
  rings.
They have unpinned my curls, let fall my hair.
My head they have razored bare.

Yesterday I lay in a warm bed that was no trouble;
Today I am naked, fallen, all a-stubble.
Yesterday plumped fingers reaped my flesh in celebration;
Today I am poured out on fallow ground, a spilled libation.

I wonder (when all was said) did she put a brazen face
  on things,
Shrugging off the taught disgrace of the noose that rings
Her leathered neck with its unbroken promise;
Or did she tongue the wind, its breath kissing her lips.

WINTER SOLSTICE

On this the shortest day of the year unspoken with
   promise I wait by the
mouth of the river beside a wood of holly

and hazel, of dwarf oak and alder, listening for the
   screech of snow
geese wintering in the estuary,

keeping watch below the shallow flight of migrants for
   the Island
of the Moon to surface on the water

face down, its drowned tongue undertowing wind and
   current.
On this the longest night of the year.

And you come with dumb sound over soft ground
   carrying on your
feet seeds from the wood,

your arms cradling broken antlers of holly clotted
with its ooze

of berry, dressing my bare lips with the worn velvet
of your mouth,

your heelprints an archipelago of moons waning
to the crescent outline of hooves.

WAKING

It is no time to wake her now
for she is rocking the baby to sleep
beside the fire
her head full of the lullaby
her arms heavy without their load
her heart nesting in the hawthorn.

It is no time to wake her now
for she is walking down the lane
between the brambles
her head full of the wind
her arms an empty shawl across her breast
her heart dropping out of its nest.

It is no time to wake her now
for she is digging a lazy bed
behind the wall
her head full of the dream
her arms are laying down
her heart halved for setting in the ground.

It will be time enough to wake her
when she comes to the blackthorn
by nightfall. For she will be tired
with the rocking and the walking and the digging
and would sleep to wake in the dark
not able to find her way home.

Gráinne Tobin

UNTIMELY

for Mary Wall

Every woman had been her best friend,
every man had planned to marry her.
The city church was full as if for Christmas.
We'd journeyed through the frozen dark for hours
to be in time for her,
who had never been early for anyone,
but was not, as prophesied, late
for her own funeral,
having taken only months
to die at thirty-three.

Already there were legends
of how she'd keep us
waiting, exhausted by expectation,
furious, duped, swearing *never again;*
then just appear, unlooked-for as an angel,
ablaze with sequinned apologies,
costumed in excuses so lustrous
it was enough to see her and be dazzled.

The funeral meal was like a wedding breakfast;
the bride, however, absent,
forever awaited,
so that in later years
we're startled by girls glimpsed in the street,
loops of fair hair and long scarves swinging by,

and turn in hope to hear her truant voice
propose some folly:
Ah, come on, sure what's your hurry?
We'll be a long time dead.

LADIES' NIGHT

A dozen women settling round a table,
in the community centre proudly
muralled in red-white-and-blue
scrolls, red hands with daggers,

unzip their winter jackets and wait
for me to give them something
they didn't know they had.
Last week it was the cooking demonstration,

tonight they're getting me, one of the other sort,
the creative writing woman, their guest
in spite of church and politics,
for I am trusted to remember

some hated school, some never learned to write.
I promise them in these two hours together
we will make a poem
pieced from all our lives.

We lay out scraps of stories on the table,
pregnancies and births – my own tale first,
a fragment from our female comedy
offered in all its colours. One decides

to risk me. She begins:
It was a military hospital,
and I a sergeant's wife.
First births are always hard,

but we sat up for officers' inspection
wearing nighties, with our army-issue babies
in their fishtank cots beside us,
the sheets perfectly folded.

It seems some password has been spoken.
In married quarters, says another,
we made love on mattresses
still wrapped in polythene

for fear of baby stains. The first three feet
of paintwork could be fingermarked,
but doortops must be polished daily
for spot checks, gardens paraded,

army wives always on duty.
Our child was nearly blinded once,
her father on manoeuvres;
they said he'd have to follow

the army or his family. He chose
to love us best. We live here now.
Legitimate targets. And she smiles at me,
over the rag-rug poem

we bind with secrecy,
names, ranks, addresses to be left behind,
remnants of these salvaged lives,
when I return to mine, the other, side.

EIGHT MONTHS GONE

Tower of ivory, house of gold, ark of the covenant . . .
Litany of the Blessed Virgin

I am your roof and shelter.
Your accommodation is the best I can offer.
I try to be the perfect host,
remembering your vitamin pills,
your afternoon naps.
But now you clumsily pace my body
in these dark hours when everyone's at rest,
ham-fisted, insomniac guest. Give you an inch
and you take a mile. Secretive stranger.

We haven't even been introduced.
I've taken you in on faith.
Not that I grudge you this lodging,
in spite of your disorderly behaviour,
waking me with lurching hiccups,
making your tight roof ripple and stretch,
my muscles strain to hold your restlessness.

One day you'll struggle out into the light,
declare yourself at last.
Meanwhile I propose peaceful coexistence.
Lie gently for a while. Soon we will meet
skin to skin, my fugitive, face to face.

RURAL RETREAT

July was worst. A young man pulled a knife
on him one evening after closing time,
the pearly sealight fading, as their roof
shook to the ladders of the bunting squad.

Often at night they would be loudly jolted
from their deep lovers' sleep by unseen fists
thumping the windowpane beside their bed,
insults in accents not yet understood.

They stuck it out, in disbelief at first.
Still the waves played along the rocky shore,
black guillemots nested in the granite harbour.
Village life takes patience, they were told.

The pounding and the jeering petered out;
soon they put right their house and bought a pram.
Bunting bloomed discreetly each July.
From fear or tact, they spent the Twelfth away.

In time the news was bad. The threats began.
Pregnant, she picked the shards of window glass
out of the toy box, and arranged to sell.
Not quite intimidation, the policeman said.

BRADFORD-ON-AVON, WILTSHIRE, AUGUST 6TH

Here is the place:
where the river runs quietly
through the cosy town,
past weavers' cottages, church and library,
pub garden and swimming baths,
under the bridge
among evening smells of leaves and water,
from the boating steps
they are floating lanterns for Hiroshima.

Silently (for my Irish voice
might tell too much)
I drop some money in the bowl,
take a home-made lantern,
join the murmuring pilgrims
at the water's edge.
Without speech, I am invisible, and listen.
The cheerful commonplaces
of their conversation
are respectful, like small talk round a graveside.
There are no speeches or announcements.

But in the thickening dusk,
ceremonially, one by one,
they light their votive candles,
set down thin craft
with paddling fingers
on the calm dark river.
The wind breathes
into the paper sails,
the lanterns glide downstream,
glowing, lit from within

against the darkness,
till the current carries them
softly out of sight.

I light my candle, float my lantern
with the rest,
watching some catch
in whorls of water,
flash and twist to ash,
their flames extinguished
like the countless dead.

AWARENESS EVENING

Speeches from the Suits go on for hours,
but the girl in the next row
has a wood nymph's neck
fringed with tendrils the colour of bark,
outgrowing last month's smart haircut.
The glossy fur
of her gorgeous olive nape
above the white crochet jacket
invites my palm – ah, only
to lay a hand, as if
to brace that stem against
the pull and snap of the incurious world.

THE WHOLE STORY

All the women in our family
like to toast their arses at the fire
in a more or less ladylike manner,
enjoying the backstage warmth of it
and the familiar soundtrack
from my father,
warning us all to be careful,
citing heredity,
for my mother's mother
set petticoats on fire in 1920 –
not once but twice,
daydreaming by the flames,
lifting long skirts behind her
till the scorched smell and the smoke
brought my grandfather leaping
to roll my young granny
in her own hearthrug,
averting oblivious combustion.

Was it quenching or courting?
Thrown gasping on the floor,
corseted in whalebone and carpet,
did my smouldering foremother
conspire in that solicitous embrace?

ELAINE GASTON

NEW YEAR'S DAY

'Keep between the hedges,' I shouted
and you laughed at the words
you had not heard for years
then drove off down the lane

to the town for some messages.
I stayed and cleared away the lunch,
fish pie with potatoes and beans,
the big mess you always made

when you were home and some new dish
was tried on our North Antrim palates.
You must have driven out the main line
past the New Year's ploughing match.

They were there from all over,
Tyrone, Fermanagh, County Down.
A frost lay on the ground
the earth was hard

but old Sammy McCormack
could plough the straightest furrow
rain, hail or shine.
On your way home it was getting dark

as you stopped in the village
for a cabbage and half a pint of cream.
If you had still lived around here
maybe you would have remembered

the ploughing match, logged it deep
with the words you used to know.
Maybe you would have remembered
the clarry of the dark country road

the big lorry parked there
six tractors on it, no lights.
You kept between the hedges
straight into the back of it.

Muck all over the windscreen
cabbage and cream all over the car
you against the steering wheel.
Now the hedges you keep between

are two lines of yew trees
we walked down six days later.
Clay freshly dug, deeper than any furrow,
you, cold, stiff as the earth they ploughed.

PUNISHMENT

They gave me a terrible drubbing one day
and sore from the sally rod
I went across the yard,
hoiked the dog up wooden rungs
into the half-loft to find dark bales,
last summer's grass and meadow flowers
fading into hay.

My story rolled over the dog
who softened to my sores,
licked my wounds. Big rough tongue.
All through the day they called me
in the yard, the cattle shed, the dairy
away out the back to the dam, the sheugh
and down the brae to the main line.
Panic rising. My name over and over.
But I sat tight as a bat in the rafters.
Revenge sweeter than the hay I lay on.

Only when the half-light fell,
only when I gleeked through the hole
in the gable end and saw the evening star
rise above the moss,
only when hunger rumbled me down the ladder
did I cross the flags to the kitchen
sturdy with artificial light.
I vied with moths cluttering at the pane
to see my mother stirring soup,
brothers and sisters hovering near.

I went in
to brave my father's footstep and his hand
but my mother's face told all:
relief would outweigh punishment.
I would be all right. Saved from one more skite.

SEASONED

He cannot bend to tie his shoe.
I stoop to make the knot
that takes me back
to when he carried fully grown men
down stairs in the middle of the night

found them in floods or snowdrifts
hauled them up cliffs on stretchers
pulled them out of sheughs and bogs
all in a day's work

he held mothers' hands in ambulances
gave the kiss of life
in porches, on roadsides
delivered babies in toilets
of country bars long after closing.

At home he bathed us on a Saturday night
bent over the tub, sleeves rolled up
arms covered in suds
told stories of him as a boy
when once he cycled twenty miles to run a race
and won, then cycled twenty home.

His back, a solid Irish oak,
bent, moved, straightened
to each particular need.
Now its knots tell the years
of a thousand people who leant on him
shoulders that carried other people's lives
as well as his own.

He cannot bend to lace his shoe
and I have learned to make the loop.

ANGEL

She came from the quarter
of the red-haired people
and she was
the waterfall of bracken
cascading down the hill
the late autumn leaves
the auburn tumbling
Pre-Raphaelite curl of hair
and freckles,

no lemon juice could dab them off
(though Granny swore it would)
the stigma from centuries deep down
rumoured gypsy blood
a fiery temper and a wild heart.

These days I see her
in my mind's eye
her face does not come
just splash of orange
spirals and triangles
filter through
then slip away

and all I know is
the red sandstone of the churchyard
the adobe presence
the iron ore of the Causeway
in the evening sun
the road at Carrowreagh
the hazel wood of her eyes
the carrot seed of her voice

and all I know is
the russet apple
the leaf turning
the flame blazing
the dappling above.

GONE

I am filling my page with your name
dancing it in the wave
seeking your seaweed smell in my bed
your juice on my sheet
your face in my rock pool
I am washing your voice on my body
over and over
plunging excitement
through a full dark ocean back
to your shining basalt

my shoulders shedding mercury
water off an oily seal
I slip into the deep with you
stir jealous geese on wild grass
splash and wet my lips with your salt
till I burst for air rising
streaming
lustre blood sweating
shells along the sand
parched
for the sense of your open hand

till the passing word is
shafts of light
on swelling seas
till the story is simply
a hard thirst:
something, anything
to tell me you were here.

BACK

After the airport's artificial light
the north Antrim night
wind that would take the face off you.
We load the car in B1 and fumble
for eighty pence car park toll.
Over ramps, past guns, checkpoints
and some poor sinner's been hauled in.
'The evenings are fairly drawing in right enough.'

We drive silent until the motorway narrows
into roads and lanes I know, familiar as your hand.
The Frosses, trees that hold up the road,
save it sinking into the bog. Big tough roots.
Yon same ETERNITY WHERE? sign
on yon same Scots pine.
'You know where you are now.'

THE WHOLE SPECTRUM

for Séan

The double rainbow
behind the gasworks
that late afternoon in September
as I drove you to work
after we made many-coloured love
in my narrow single bed

the double rainbow
the light drizzle across the Lagan
the wild fire sunset behind Cave Hill
and the way we had to pull into the kerb
to take it all in.

THE LIE OF THE LAND

for Shauna

Your laugh a curlew's call
in the back room where we sit
to the wee small hours.
Stories our mothers told us

stories, our own
ramble off, stop
at every hole in the hedge
diverge, converge again.

Small roads through the bog
townlands in our minds
each with their own
particular story.

Phrases turn like a sod
words churn like the butter
we used to know
as we roll and heuch

slap rowdy hands on thighs.
Wild and expansive as our history
we try to find again
the lie of the land

different words for different fields
fallow, meadow, ploughed.
New paths through old tracks
opening blocked roads.

ANN ZELL

AT THE GROSVENOR ROAD ROUNDABOUT

for Nina

Verdigris copper domes, disengaged
from their squat certainties, redeem
the wreck of a skyline owing more
to urban renewal than to bomb blasts.

Tarmac denial of texture. Fume of lorries
grumbling past the maelstrom I wait to enter,
bike resting against a border of bricks
in tough earth colours, where no earth is.

I lift up my eyes to Cave Hill
from whence cometh no help. Pretend
the most vigilant woman I know is
not on a morphine drip in another city

but back hill-walking in Glencolumbkille.
Where it is raining and the sun is shining
and either/or logic is blowing away
with the mist over Slieve League.

LAMENT FOR A LOST FRAGMENT OF ANTRIM COAST AMMONITE

It looked worked. A ridged, curved segment
of something heavy as iron
without the taste or smell of iron.

Rubbed hard between my hands, its matt brown surface
took on the sheen of a bronze age artefact
or the lustre it might have had in nature,
if it was natural.

The expert said it was definitely pre-Celtic;
a free-swimming cephalopod from the early Cretaceous,
preceding by a hundred million years
the middle stone age tribe who came to manufacture
    flints
and trade stories with the bees, settling
near the shore where they could remember other homes.

I wanted a talisman to bind me to this shore.
Lost, it is whole again – a perfect horn of Jupiter,
spiral, compacted time.
My fingers ache for its stone substance.

FOSSIL FUEL

This peat leaves umber ash so fine
the slightest displacement of air
could start an avalanche, and I kneel

holding my breath and the dustpan brush
weighed down by centuries of residue,
waiting for it to settle.

When we were short of cash before the war
she leached wood ash for lye to mix
with the rendered lard from home-killed pigs

– her laundry soap would take the skin off a baby.
Her hands were soft on Sundays.
We knew she had been raised for better things.

She told her parents she married my father
because he made her laugh. My apostasy made her cry.
I kept an ocean and a continent between us.

The last trip home, with not much said my brother
drove me out by the twin buttes across the river, where
she waited for my father to come and call her name.

Mormons get to be gods if they've been good.
Eternity as a good god was more than I could fathom.
I wanted endings. Once around is enough.

I'm the same age my mother was, kneeling
like she did so often with no loss of dignity,
wondering if I'll make old bones.

WATER RITES

The night before I left home it was our turn
for the water. A grown girl he couldn't deal with
I was no longer my father's daughter.
He asked me along as a farewell gesture.

We went through the fields single file, not talking.
He dug away the earth dams blocking the ditches
where he wanted the water to go, while I
said my goodbyes to scenes of child labour.

The canal was quicksilver in the moonlight, high
with runoff from a storm in the mountains,
feeding unused water back into the river
and all the way to the imagined sea.

When it was time I levered up the headgate at his
say-so, and watched the ditchbed fill with light;
the curl and push of water down the furrows
etching the nearest field in lines of light.

He leaned on his shovel gauging the flow, a man
who'd plowed and planted seed and provided water.
Acolyte at his midnight mystery, I was closer
to him in the silence than I'd been for years.

But I was impatient to start my exile –
eager for a place where the lights of traffic
would map networks of city streets; where
there'd be so many words they could be squandered –

and I came away easily, no more attached to the land
than a sapling before its taproot finds the water
table. Now, when rain releases the scent
locked in dry soil, nostalgia tricks me.

Intimately connected to the earth
I'm playing in the dust near my working
father. I run to him for a skinned knee
and the hurt won't heal. Kisses can't make it better.

EXPEDITION

He shows me footprints of a four-toed lizard
preserved in Permian sediment, revealed
by the Colorado's open-heart surgery.

I learn Coconino sandstone, the lizard's climate,
the time of day the tracks were made.
How we can know it was going up, not down, the dune.

We are as remote from each other as we are
from the lizard. Across a major unconformity
our slow geological talk discovers

evidence for a lizard-quick boy, a girl
who followed him through sagebrush and irrigation
ditches, before the future crystallised.

I find a cast. He names and dates it.
Playing at palaeontology
I follow my brother down the Hermit Trail.

SCOTTISH POETRY LIBRARY
5 Crichton's Close
Edinburgh EH8 8DT
Tel: 0131 557 2876

OVERLOAD

The crescent moon
pulls a ripple of water up the beach
tenuous as clingfilm
sheen on the sand
doubling the inlet rocks' solidity
against an insubstantial sky.   All day
I've been gathering sensations
greedy for after-images. Not knowing
like an overstimulated child
how much I needed the night.

INTERLUDE

So well camouflaged I took it for
driftwood, weathered pine –
the grey seal pup coffined between
two rocks on Derrylahan beach. Perfectly
water-shaped, a long *Oh*
that could have slipped down its mother's birth canal
without trauma.

I come here to forget, to remember
white summers, Fergus singing the seals in,
all of us basking under an enchantment.

Eyes wide.   Not a mark on it.   Flippers
folded decorous as hands
over the sand-silver feathered satin
fur. Laid out by the tide ready for viewing.

The doctor from Düsseldorf who
would live here if she didn't live there
even after we rounded the corner and came upon
a bloated sheep, legs in the air, being
disembowelled by a gang of hooded crows,
gobbets of wool scattered like bog cotton
over the emerald turf, said

Slieve League seen from the sea
was 'not worse' than the Cliffs of Moher. It
reminded me of the abstract expressionist mural
on the Lenadoon wall of Woodbourne barracks.

She would never go to Belfast. I would
never go to Germany while they burn unwanted
guests.   Standoff.   We agreed on nature.

ANNIVERSARY MARCH

A millipede.   Or actors in a budget film
stepping in place while the backdrop is scrolled past.
The last open field on the road comes by.
Two piebald horses and a boy on a motorbike race
up and down, up and around, patterning the long grass.
The unmuffled noise of the bike mixes
with the whump-growl-whine of helicopters
and the off-key fluting of the nearest band.

The boy waves to his friends, pretending he is
herding the horses. Dogging the heels of the march,
mechanised cowboys with plastic-bullet guns
gun their engines as we stop for stragglers,
pretending they are herding us down the road.
We move only when we are ready, along a route
our feet have memorised; family groups
keeping no order, keeping the children close.

Often photographed but seldom seen
we appear no better and no worse than
other people, on the rare occasions
when our film is screened. It is not apparent
that we are also with the horses
whose manes and tails float on the slipstream
of their running. Who gallop out of the frame
and up towards the mountain as the footage ends.

NATURE PROGRAMME

Before there were helicopters
    there were dragonflies.
Seagulls exploiting the updrafts
    circled like spotter planes.
Owls probed the night
    with infra-red eyes.

I dream of teleported fauna
    from the South American pampas:
nonvegetarian capybaras,
    armadillos the size of armoured cars,
anteaters specialising
    in soldier ants.

Before there were helicopters
    there were dragonflies.
And will be, after.

MARGARET CURRAN

THAT'S LIFE

On Blunderbuss Road
By chance I met Aimee Pilchard.
We walked past the high field
And saw, instead of haystacks,
Giant spools of hay
Lying haphazard where they'd rolled.

Aimee rolled as she walked.
Her heavy hips swayed and swung
With every step she took;
Or when she laughed good-naturedly,
Which was often.

Aimee looked at the golden spools
And shook with laughter.
We both laughed so much
We fell down and around
On the grass, helpless and aching.

Then we threaded daisy chains
And walked back to the village
Hand in hand, when we were ten
And I was thin.

AFTER THE FUNERAL

I walk among angels
With sooty shawls and chipped wings.
Signposts abound
In wood, granite and Italian marble
On properties lovingly maintained
Weed-free with stone chippings and everlasting flowers.
The warm afternoon floats away
The noise of distant traffic.

All have equal rest and rights here
Except the south side is a little warmer
And butterflies linger longer
On the wild nettled patch
Where paupers lie.
And old wreaths wither,
Their *Fondest Love* notes
Weathering.

I come upon a gardening son
Tidying up his mother's place
With small trowel and neat clippers.
He tells me simply:
'Yes, I come often – though she's not here.'
Pause to search my face for attitudes.
'We believe in the Resurrection . . .'

Strange echo of that other gardener Mary met.

TEMPORARY BREAK IN TRANSMISSION

Cars have breakdowns.
Celebrities too,
For publicity.
But not ordinary flat-footed
Dull-witted, nose-to-grindstone
Me.

This is worse than Dutch elm disease,
Canker, and dry rot put together.
I'd rather have two broken legs and an arm
Than dwell in this joylost
Blighted place.

Things seemed right until one long sad day
Drawn into weeks
Cracks appeared in the egg
And I was afraid to look out
Into alienland.
Isolate.

Others beckon and throw
Comfort and lifelines which don't reach
Me, thinking on quicksand
Sinking in a bottomless sea.

They say it will pass.
'All things pass away.'
So I'm gone forever then?
'Course not,' they smile.
'Keep taking the tablets.'

THE HAT BOUGHT FOR SPAIN

This year she took a wild notion
Like a foolish last fling
To visit the unknown, real Spain.
Not Costa Bananas, or Costa Discos
Where tourists are packed in egg-box hotels,
But the richly mysterious Spain –
Where a Murillo boy plays pipes outside a mosque
For his audience of white doves

And secret treasures in Cádiz are revealed
Deep underground, the air so cool, still, suspended
It echoes the human voice fifteen times.
Visitors awe and wonder aloud, ALOUD, ALOUD
At priceless silver chalices, diamond-inlaid crosses
And golden glowing vestments, gifts from the Incas.

She thrilled at the great deep ravine in Arcos.
For Whom the Bell Tolls was filmed here
(In schooldays she longed to be Ingrid Bergman).
On the red mountains tortuous olives grow,
Their black branches imploring, yearning towards the
     sun,
Like the wild tormented lovesongs of Flamenco dancers.
Golden plains of wheat stretch to the skyline,
Swaying before warm breezes from Morocco . . .

The hat hangs around the house now in various places,
Its gold shining straw spilling Spanish sunshine.
There's another notion forming in her mind –
'That hat could be worn in Turkey, or even India . . .
Why keep a hat if you're not going to wear it?'

HEARTBURN

Cod liver oil for the lungs
Sennapod tea on Saturdays
And, darkly ominous,
Castor oil, if necessary.
Children should be seen and not heard.
Grown-ups, it seemed, knew all the rules.

Visiting stiffly on Aunt Emma's prickly horsehair sofa,
Small legs straight out, I watched her
Shine the range to silver for Jack's coming.

Yet,
Home from the shipyard smoking his pipe
Her Jack spat on the range, often, carelessly.
The spits sizzled, hopped, danced dry
While Aunt Emma burned angrily.

Then she and Jack wouldn't 'speak'.
The range roared; the gas mantle flared and hissed.
Perhaps, like children, anger should be seen but not
   heard.

He took his lovely greyhounds out
For long lonely walks
And fed them good steak.

Aunt Emma in thin high voice
Told the empty air,
'He loves them dogs more than me',
And fiercely mangled the heavy washing

In her clean whitewashed yard.
She lost the top of one finger that way. . .

Yet,
She and Jack smiled so happily
In their parlour wedding photo.
I didn't know why a range was so important.

UNMARRIED DAUGHTER

Her pallid face,
Small bird of fluttering hope
Trapped in the window,
She swept a dead fly off the sill.
Pink petals fell from pot-bound geraniums
Into the wastepaper bin.

The woman by the fire was old,
Immutable, fixed as rock.
'Who was that?' she peeved.
'No one,' sighed the girl.
'Well, draw the curtains,
We don't want them looking in.'

The girl turned away.
'Yes, Mother.
I'll get the tea
And fix your bed.'
From the fire fell a living coal;
Flickering uncertainly, it died.

JOAN NEWMANN

AT KRASI

for Kate

An ancient plane tree – filigree shadows –
Twelve strong men cannot
Surround its girth – water
Colder than snow –
And Irene, meaning peace –
Her taverna up in the branches
Of almonds and figs and ripening apricots –
Vines springing new green grapes
Above our airy heads – wine from the barrel –
A salad as high as the mountain top
We're hugged against –
Bread – warm grain smell of the sun –
Pale red wine trickling from wood –
A day so poured full to running over
That twelve strong men couldn't get their arms
Around it.

THE APOSTLES

for Hazel and Nicola

KIRIA VANGELIA
The Goat Woman

Vangelia leads the goat, who knows,
White and mighty in the pink light of falling night,
She's going home: her two kids dance
Silliness of young unwary things.
It has been the rain drawing green
From baked clay; faith in growing things
That brings Vangelia to wash her face,
Reach for coins earned from goat's cheese
For beeswax candles flickering
Affirmation in the night procession.
She walks the dark, foot-tread sure as a goat.

KIRIA KATERINA
Water Music

She sits with bare unconscious knees
Like a woman playing the cello in private,
Her grandmother's hands paddling a dish of suds,
She immerses the clothes
Seeing to their needs:
Music in the bountiful flow
Of pure and running water.

KIRIA ANNA
Covering

On the morning of the Resurrection
She sought a tin of white paint,
An old hardened brush,
To cover the earth brown of the table
With a shroud of stunning white.
White on her black pinafore.
She will put on her Easter clothes
For church; the table naked in air,
A resting place for yellow breeze-blown flowers
Of the spring-glorious acacia tree.

KIRIA ARGIRO
Lady of the Flowers

From her faded green doorway
She feels the need of her geraniums,
Spilling and blooming cerise,
Crimson, pink, peach, purple,
For cooling water before
Midday sun burns round.
She lifts their heads,
As carefully as a mother
Raising a full cup to the mouth of a child:
Water caught to the last drip
Poured as libation on thirsty roots.

KIRIA FRONI
The Cook

His blood-red comb jerks
His squawks of consternation:
Light working miracles on feathers
Bronze, amber, copper, gold.
Froni pinions his helpless wings;
His humiliated feet, a dirty yellow,
Lift from red solid earth,
Scratch warm shimmering air.
Froni carries a shining worn knife.
His beak gapes, disbelieving eyes
Aghast at his own Easter dying.

KIRIA ANGELIKI
The Girl Who Weeps

Her eyelids raw with sorrow for her brother,
Coming from the crying with the women,
A piece of funeral bread, sweet and pungent
As incense blended in honey,
Careless in her hand.
She is blackness – her hair, her clothes, her eyes
Fixed on the finite past.
Sun, warm as a hand held out in concern
Cannot bring itself to touch her.

KIRIA VASSILIKO
Lamb's Intestines

It is a knowledge stored from Easter
To Easter – like the dipping of long beeswax candles –
She draws from the water fleshy rope of lamb's
    intestines,
Winding them on the small delicate hoof
That rested so surely
On scent of trampled flowers.

KIRIA ANDONIA
The Housekeeper

In the orange and yellow wealth
Of the garden of the house circled by wall
Where Kazantzakis wrote his letters,
She comes wringing out her mop
Rubbing her lower back with a wet hand.
The midday sun raises up her enduring face.
She sees without seeing artichokes, geraniums.
Among the Easter lilies she squats,
Draws up white knickers brighter than light,
Picks a lemon, brings its essence to her nose,
Leaves the tree juddering to a standstill,
The tremor caught up in the ringing of the bells.

KIRIA MARIA
Mother and Child

Under mauve jacaranda blooms comes the woman,
Soft-moving as shadow, all her body strains with weight
Of carrying her disabled daughter
Whose head hides on her neck.
Only child's eyes recoil from hostile glances
Of people drifting towards the church bell
Which tells her mother,
'That child is a manifestation of evil' –
'That child is the visitation of the sins of the fathers' –
'That child ought to be kept out of human sight' –
'That child is a judgment of God' –
'That child should not have been born'.

KIRIA ELENI
The Gatherer

The shock of green on her shoulder,
Her widow's sun-bleached black clothes,
Hair hidden beneath a black scarf,
She pauses before taking the shortest road home;
Adjusts the stack of animal fodder
– Vine trimmings, grasses, wilted wild flowers –
Steps across pale sand
Around oiled bodies greedy for Easter sun;
Sets her censoring eye beyond sea
Spilling its froth on slippery rock,
Out to mauve, pale turquoise
Of a heat-hazed, peopleless horizon.

KIRIA THALIA
The Provider

With an angry mattock she pounds soil
Hard as baked terracotta pottery shards,
Bends to lift stones,
Bends to scatter seed, cover seed.
On her side she rests, her dusty hands
Clasped beneath her wrinkled cheek,
Against wood of an angular settle,
Her white knees above black knee socks
Below a black cotton skirt;
Stilling the ache of effort.
Her eyes, her bones, her skin
Watchful for signs of rain.

KIRIA SOPHIA
The Baker

Easter biscuits glisten gold with olive oil,
Their hollow centres – a koulouri – a well
Which must not turn dry;
Their hollow centres
Stone hewn from rock – death in mind –
The hallowed sepulchre.
Fire is swept aside in a clay oven –
Small circles of dough are slid
Towards the heat. Sophia
Times, in the rhythm of her blood,
The moment of their rising.

KIRIA ATHENA
Crochet

Fine white cotton unwinds for the feel of her fingers,
Her eyes recall without reminder – spaces, loops, knots:
Sleight of hand hooking flowers, netting birds.
Crochet filigree bunched on her lap.
Last stitch – her strong teeth bite dry through thread.
She holds – a filter for the evening light
Her exquisite creation – intently –
Spreads its radiant harmony on a chair back,
Turns to dormant yarn, steel needle – still warm.

SALLY WHEELER

AUTUMN RITUAL

Oak leaves in my breast
White wool on my arm
I go through the wood
Stalking the dead.
Leaves fly above; underfoot,
Crackle like golden foil.
The ruined graveyard gapes on the left.
I am ready to sing, to confess
All I have done, left undone.
White strings of incense fume
Against my black dress.
Where is the grave I must honour?
All seems small and lost,
The names on the stones unknown.
I must fall far from the tree,
Pierce the mud like an arrow;
Split open the green inedible husk
To show the shining fruit.

ANCESTRAL VOICES

'70 IN THE SHADE 1ST AUGUST '46'
Carved on the bricks
Pale in the glare;
Bright fever of postwar.
Music drifts from an open door;
A scent of hops against the wall.
Sudden shadows fall,
Flit batlike over the grass;
Jets balancing on thunder
That seconds after
Splits the skies;
Relentless Valkyries,
Shapes of death hatched deep
In metal caves of ceaseless gale,
Whose voice in sleep
Invades my dreaming mind;
'You must marry the North Wind.
You must marry the North Wind.'

NIGHT HAUNTING

Phone ringing in the callbox;
Bird in a glass cage
Calls one who will not answer.

Moon riding thin clouds;
Wind stirring bare boughs
Sweeps along dead leaves.

I skim the silent streets
To knock on your window;
Need lifts me above the ground.

I rattle the latch,
Tap on the glass like hail;
Are you sleeping alone?

Poor ghost, a word can lay me
Powerless in the gutter,
Washed down it like rain.

You may turn from me, but I
Cannot be free; I am tied
To your heels like a shadow.

I look at the crack round your door;
I am so slight
I can slide beneath it.

I rise up the stair like mist
To hover by your bed;
You do not wake.

I bite my wrist so the blood
Falls on your sleeping face;
You lick your lips and smile.

I creep into the space
Between you and another,
A cold draught down your back.

You frown in sleep and rolling over
Melt my ice beneath you;
Your pillow is wet with my tears.

The heat of your skin devours me.
I have become nothing
But the echo of a dream

That wakes you and is gone.
You wash me away
Like a stain from your memory.

WOMANTREE

Flowering tree, whose branches grow
Tangled together by the wind,
Overladen, waving wild,
I stand beside you in the storm,
Feet at your roots, head in your leaves,
Trying to save your brittle stems,
Willing them to grow straight, be tall,
Not trail their flowers on the ground.
But the wind twists them from my hands;
Their petals stream out on the air,
As a girl shakes back from her face
The living burden of her hair.
Free of my fears, the branches sing
Of other flowers, another spring.

AT THE GARDEN GATE

Drawing the curtains in the early dusk,
I see two women at the garden gate,
Clothed in blue, leaning together
In a conspiracy of caring
For my neighbour, long ill, and now dying –
Their dim bending forms like rocks or trees
Like the sorrowing women
Coming to wash and bind the tortured body,
Having no thought about a risen one;
Coming at dawn with spices and linen
Through the grey still garden
To find the stone was rolled away.

TROJAN WOMEN

These lines of weeping women,
Their children dazed with exhaustion,
Leaving behind old people calm in shock
Under the stumps of trees planted for shade
Outside the matchwood of their homes;
Driving animals, pushing carts laden
With babies and household gods,
On unknown roads where every rock
May hide the enemy,
Not daring to look back;
These have walked out of history
From burning Troy,
Across wastelands of hundred-year wars,
Out of poisoned marshes and deserts,

Deep forests felled and ruined towns.
Their faces are like ours,
Not sculpted, painted or drawn;
With no heroic ancient names –
Andromache, Cassandra, Hecuba;
Their children are blond, were once well-fed,
Had toys, played games, watched TV;
And now come on it every night
Into our living-room. I switch off the set;
Think; what would I take on that long walk?
A far-off murmur grows out in the street.
We are all Trojan women now.

LOST AT SEA

To miss today the wind
Combing the grass, the field
Running like water, clouds
Caught in bare trees against the sky
New-washed after the storm;
White scraps of gulls blown
Above black rocks; the sun's
Flare on the sea; the boats
Fidgeting at anchor, masts
Tinkling with halyards.

To be lost to land,
Though ringed by islands
Fringed with reeds,
Hands grasping for ground
Empty of all but water, then air;
Hair combed by the tide, found

Caught in the weeds,
Setting the gulls screaming,
And raised at last,
Heavy as rocks onshore.

Or never to come home;
Always to be out there,
Under the lough that lies
Across the view solid as brass –
Flecked with dark fin or rock
Reaching an arm to break
Through the sea's skin –
White foam like a face
Gasping for air –
So that the watchers ache,
Holding their breath.

Lying awake at night
They hear the wind shake
The unfastened door;
Each rattle, each scrape
On shingle, a stumbling step
Jerks them upright
Heart thudding, to fall back
Again into the dark
Pressing unbroken over the lost
Who miss today,
Who are for ever missed.

OPEN AND SHUT

When love rose like the sun
She had no fear;
She ran towards it
Hands open, eyes shut,
Arms held out wide
As if to catch
Its burning sphere;
And never thought
That sleepless nights
Would make her watch
With open eyelids
Dry beyond tears;
That life would pin
Her arms down to her sides,
Closing her hands to fists;
Or through the years
Silence would spin
Its web across her mouth
Sealing her voice within,
Choking her heart;
For her love's sun had set.

MARY TWOMEY

WINTER

This is the season
I've waited for.
Trees latticed against sky
open to question.
Water chill and clear
enough to see through,
the air shrill with cold.
Sounds carry for miles.

'I must divide the alpines,'
I hear you say.
'The gardening programme
says to do it now.' But then
you conveniently forget.
The saxifrage unrolls itself
in a smothering evergreen
carpet of rosettes and cushions
and hummocks.

Snow falls steadily
contorting the delicate
framework of my trees,
making you smile.
You, the lover of pods and bark,
pelts and fleece,
remarking on how the snow finds
every nook and every cranny.
You, the lover of ice,

congratulating yourself on how
like a carapace it is
on the water-lily pond.

I break the ice
with a stick.
Let the water
flow over my
frozen fingers.

TROUT

And you [write] for the revelation . . . of some strange
unguessed-at other world . . . the towers in the water not the
air, the drowned roses and flying fish . . .

A. S. Byatt, *Possession*

A conspiracy
of fish and water.
Lambent he slumbers
stirs awake
curves legato
in soundless
lazy glides
scarcely breaking water skin.

Sinuous he arcs
in a great siphoned
leap to pierce
the gauziness of air,
touch the molten sun
the icicle moon.

Returns to browse
in jungle water weed,
to brood on stratospheres
scarcely glimpsed.

Eventually he shudders
into new life,
grasps the strung red berry,
the blood-red berry,
surges quicksilver towards
the insistent light,
implodes in
splintered radiance,
asphyxiates in air
as thick as cloth.

Prone he lies
beside the flickering flame
the dark red berry
gripped in his torn mouth,
his blood-red mouth.
Sheds scales of silver
on the smouldering ash.
Becomes a glimmering girl.

EXCHANGES IN ITALY

Do you remember
how I made you sit
as still as marble
with closed eyes?
Festooned you with
grapes and apricots
a peach in either
outstretched hand
pomegranates on
your knees
green leaves
in your hair?
There was a straw
Chianti at your feet.
We drank straight
from the bottle.

Morning . . . we
watched the jewellers
on the Ponte Vecchio
unpadlock their shutters
nail-studded like
dungeon doors.
I still wear the
ring you gave me
made of string.

You showed me goblets
of lapis lazuli
vases of rock crystal
with silver lips.
We walked through
cool dark tunnels
of ilex and cypress.
Lizards lay motionless
on hot dry stones.
Heat rose, fierce
and tremulous.

When at last
I did allow
you to speak,
your words were
chalcedony and
pearl that I
have hoarded
to myself.

SORTING

I change colour
A Painted Lady assuming its background
Blending with you
In a familiar shade
Scarcely maintaining quintessence yet
Touch me
The nub still palpable.

I change shape
Sheet water in an unaccustomed mould
Calm-shot surface
Proteus-shaped yet
Listen to me
Underneath
I gurgle and purl surreptitiously.

I change size
Swell and ebb with the moon
For lunary reasons
Drawn endlessly towards and away from you
Equilibrium forever on the turn. Yet
Look at me
In the wane
I wax.

CALDRAGH IDOL

Here I squat for ever
in wet fern and
fallen stones.
A celebration of all
things possible.

Past and future are
present in me.
I see before and after,
rimmed lozenges for eyes,
cryptic as tombs.
You cannot tell what
I am thinking.
I am the open-ended solution.

You scrutinise my
stony heart-shaped faces.
A native Janus challenging
a catechism of answers.
My scrupulous mouths are
mute and reconciled.
I am the power of suggestion.

My long arms
make diagonals to
protect myself from you.
Put your doubting hand
in the cavity
once brimful of
blood offerings to a
heartless Celtic god.

I am a Dark Age karma
aloof on my Boa Island.
I am the still stone in
the havoc of time.

SEA WALK

for Shauna and Deirdre

Your nails
the violet pearly lining
of a mussel shell.
Your closed eyes
the colour of brown
curved limpets.
Your hair on linen
laid out as thick
as seaweed.

I was afraid to touch
the whiteness of
your face.
My brave face had
all gone with you.
Kept watch beside
your stillness,
speechless as you,
the scent of lilac
through the window,
children's voices from
a summer street.

The sea roar drowns
the seagulls' screech.
I turn my ear into
the wind's sough to
pitch your voice.
I return with a
handful of campion,
a pocketful of shells.
I will never get used to your silence.

AUTISTIC

You uncurl from me like a fern
    They look with curious eyes
Curl back into yourself
    They teach themselves Makaton
When I ask you for bread
    They ask Does he take sugar?
You give me a stone
    They give you a wide berth
You and I drink tea with them
    We are bound by the unfamiliar.

EOIN'S HAIKU

If you smile I shall
part the bright wave for you, be
a lamp to your feet.

PIA GORE

TRACTOR TO GLENAAN

for Marian and Geraldine

The peatcomb
Bounced in the trailer,
Big brown hailstones,
Our eyes flooded and
Carried them downstream,
Red as severed gills
They winked and fluttered.
Daddy's head was grey as a seal;
It punched holes in the horizon
And when it dropped
The big holes healed.

Our knuckles
Whitened on the edge –
Fearful of being
Expelled by a wooden
Boot up the ass
Or killed.

We were rattled and shaken,
Three cold coins
In a savings glass.
'I hate this damned peat,
The black snails,
And the way we must compete
With the men on the opposite bank.'

What did it matter what
We said, Daddy was
Bouncing in oblivion,
Moss and castles in his head.
Later when he was dead
And we three went our different ways
I understood –
There were worse things
Than peat and snails
To claim a woman's days.

SHE IS

More pagan. He cuts
The hawthorn tree and smiles.
She guards her fears
Until they bolt like cats
To claw her heart.
He scents her
Like an onion to the core,
Creates her.
She is his
Myth, fact and dream commingled.
Each wall she breaks
Knits like a scar,
Each slain self lives
To appal her,
Her shoes are not made to fit her feet
But her feet created to fit the shoe,
Her hand to fit the glove,
Her mind to accommodate.
'We are one,

We are one,'
He whispers across the divisions.
'Define me, don't define,'
She calls from the precipice.

Now
Singular voices
Pierce the dark
More familiar and remote
Than his.

She cannot reach them,
She cannot reach them.

OLD QUARRELS

Take our words off
This merry-go-round.
They have begun to speak,
Even when our lips are
Clenched on the dark
And our minds
Have left them behind.

They are unbearable,
Stretched like catapults
To strike.

Our pockets are filled
With hard facts,
The stone ammunition
Aimed to break each pause.

STREET PATROL

Their feet pass
Silently,
And mine pass,
And occasionally
Our eyes meet
By accident.
The street shadows
Have eaten his face
And the light has
Given him mine.

Now . . . I half expect
His head to open
Like a red rose
And his heart
To stop
Like a printing machine,
The whites of his eyes
Laid bare
And blank as a sheet.

BETWEEN ME AND MY GUARDIAN ANGEL

I'm in love with the romance of poetry, she said,
In love with the *joie de vivre* of poetry,
Tell me how to write poetry.

I tell her

I fly to Montmartre
I fly to the Bec de Gaz on the Rue Montparnasse.
Place my host-white sheets
Between my vin rouge and crème de menthe.
Hold my Parker between my finger and thumb
And await the Nestlé cream of ideas,
The tomato purée of thought.

I tell her

I fly to the heart of a lotus
A queen bee, my third eye focused
On the striped worker backs of monotony.

Shush! . . .

Between me and my guardian angel
Truly I am poised
Between the Kerrygold
And Kerr Pinks
In the Rue Mortar Bombs
In the scullery making champ
Between scallions and
The udders of a Charollais
Between the lead pellets of liberation
My host-white sheets
Disappearing under the figure eight
Of potato skins.

TANYA'S ARRIVAL

Down without water
Down like a fish
Across stone.
In a darkness
Which walls each eye
And opens like
A slit tent to
Daylight.
Black, bloodied
Head thrusting
Into white
Unimaginably
Perfect.

It seems as if
My entrails
Followed her out
Into a metal bowl
Held up like a church plate.
There is nothing
But white, stiff white
Starched friction
Whipped from beneath.
A red pond
Blotting across sheets.

The creaking white
Feet whispering
In and out
Like the rubber fingers,
Red hot pokers
Scented of womb.

KATE NEWMANN

FEMALE TIGER ESCAPES FROM BELFAST ZOO,
    13 JANUARY 1994

When I need to pray
I look for a miracle
In the water grey height
Of a heron,
Try not to think of the savage impossibilities
Staring back through bars
At the she-tiger.

Once, with other children,
I stood,
Repelled by her desperation,
Dulled fur and crazed
Pads indifferent to concrete –
Such a small space that
Every ugly inch was intimate –
Mucoused eyes that had met
So many glances
They knew them as a concrete wall.

Only humiliation left,
She hurled herself
From one side
To the other side –

Iron shadows thrown across her back
Like railway sleepers
In sinister animation –
Forwards and backwards
Careful not to tread a circle,
Defying rhythm and shape,
Jarring and jerking heavy limbs
In case a latent memory
Should betray her into a moment of beauty,
Or surrender.

Like a cat ingesting its young
She had absorbed her self
Into this carcass
Which could only keep unstill,
Her own coat caging her.

This morning she is not there.
Men speak of draining the moat
Which stagnated quietly
Around her.
No one says that tigers can swim.

I stifle the growling fear
That she hoped beyond
Her compound for
An other place to be.

I cannot find a prayer for her.
It is winter.
The herons have stayed away.

PASIPHAË SAT, OLD AND IN BLACK

I was young
And very beautiful.
If you had seen –
Breasts like lemons,
Minos used to say.
Very beautiful.

But . . . thus it ends.
I saw the bull
And I loved that moment.
I loved him – the way he was.
I understood Europa well then.
Beautiful – white
With long eyelashes above
His big eyes
And soft skin
On his chest, between his legs.
If you had touched.

Well, I said to him,
'I love you' – but he didn't understand
He didn't understand
Because a bull he was.
Thus, to have him
I had to become a cow.
Eh . . .

They made me a cow
With wood and I got inside
But I didn't like it.
Very hard – my knee
Hurt the way I was.
And it smelt of resin –

My smell couldn't be smelt
And I couldn't be seen.
But I waited, I waited.
I couldn't
Go to him – I couldn't.
I could only stand like that –
Wood.

And he came, and he got on top of me
But I didn't feel anything.
Only his thing.
I couldn't touch the fur
On his chest, or stroke
His eyelashes
Or hold on to his horns
Which I had thought would be good.
And quickly it ended.

Nor the white could I see
And I only faintly heard
Hot breath from his soft nostrils –
Like silk.

And I was beautiful – but
A bull he was and he didn't understand.
Wood I had to become in order to have him.
He only loved the wooden cow.
But if I hadn't got in
He would have crushed me likely.

Eh . . . thus it is.
And I had the child, bad fate,
And it was not well . . .
But . . . if the gods want . . .
What can we do. . . .

MOTHER EARTH MOTHER GODDESS

Moulded of biscuit clay,
Grounded in assurance,
Eyes open to every sight,
Neck extended, flaunting fragility,
Defying destruction,
And long coiling arms
Cupping all hope,
Promising the earth.

The vessel on my arm echoes
Hollow conch calls.
Barefoot you came to me
Across floors
Of broken seashells
And I could not
Lift you
Out of reach
Of the undertow.

Pottery words
Cannot hold
Such hopeless matter.
Shattered into shards,
Pieced together,
No seeming is intact.

Unworthy metamorphosis
Formed me
From sandy worm casts –
Wound and unwound
In pelvic spirals
Of dust,
A contraction of tree rings.

I emerged from ash
No phoenix,
But a pithos,
An unreliable cocoon,
Overturned and underground,
Gaping at the travesty of delivery,
The dry wait,
The unbearable space.

SEA HORSES

'I wish you could make me pregnant'
He said.
I see us bellying in the green,
Growing tentacles like plants
To disguise our extraordinary beings,
Living to the irresistible pull
Of Moon and Tide;
Beyond the flux
We do not ebb and flow,
Ours a more essential surge,
Rippling into thousands of lunar young,
Cocooned in a paternal pouch,
Released, effortless, fully formed,
Relinquished at once to fend for themselves,
To respond to the rhythms
Which for now
Lull us into peace,
Nerve ends still as the seaweed
We have partially become.

RECLAMATION

I was thinking of the Zuider Zee

               When your sister told me

Its salt-tamed, cold-bordered blue

               That you had gone to Holland

Of Elvira on a bus from Lelystad hospital

               You were living with a woman

Her husband was ill

               You had told your wife and son

She was having to sell her precious stone collection

               You had never felt so free

She had told her husband

               Free from past and future

She hated the polders

               And you had left for Holland

It was unnatural

               To live with a young woman

Sooner or later the land would sink back

               For good.

MY MOTHER AND I PAINTING GALWAY BAY

Trying, failing, to float my mind out to sea,
Think solid cold into the wash my boulders had
   melted to,
My wall become horizon, my sea sky,
My mountains lunging water brown in waves,
A blurred intrusion . . .
I wandered to the petrol blue,
Military green,
The camouflage spectrum my father had chosen
For us – muted, grounded, slightly sullied –
To see the world
(The other paints cost more,
He could see no difference)
– Mustard brown –
Colours for a wet day on the Yorkshire Dales,
Not the turbulent bite of Atlantic rain.
We added cadmium yellows and made do.

RUTH CARR

EXILE

Out here
in the eye of the storm
needle-threading is
art and survival.

By the sheltering glow
of your fire
I can't even see
needle's eye.

We stab more than stitch
in rhyme more than rhythm
and nothing is sewn
into one.

Sinking sun
runs rivers of gold from my eyes,
my child born under a blanket
of stars in a seamless sky.

WE SHARE THE SAME SKIN

for my mother

We shared the same skin, your touch
home to my body. To grow up
I built walls, defining
where you ended and I began.

It was a child sulking to shut
you out. You waited, a quiet
stream for me to surface in.
That's where to find you now –

hunkered down on a river bank
needle or pencil in hand, sometimes
pins in your mouth, sometimes humming,
or leant against some stubborn

wind-spent tree. You showed me that
obvious thing – that under the skin
there's human, that dressing-up is
a game fit only for children.

That obvious thing paid lip-service to
but nobody does – you did it most times,
shared your skin with so many
I needed to know you loved

me more than any old refugee.
I walled up inside, let my body
go begging for crumbs like poor Tom,
a craving that couldn't find centre.

But we shared the same skin
and when yours grew too tired
and too yellow to care –
with a child of my own but still

not grown up – I couldn't let go
until prodigal waters burst
mortar from brick, I broke through
to your salt-bedded river.

We share the same skin, my daughter
and me. She's building walls
to define where I end
and she can make a beginning.

HANGING TREE

In the featherless heart of a night plucked bare
I hear what the crows have been calling
for hundreds of years.
I hear with an unstopped ear

'Caught in the tree, caught in the tree,
tongue of a woman with healing spells.
Calling the wind, calling the moon,
calling on me to peck her free.'

YOUR BLUE NORWEGIAN CAP

Your blue Norwegian cap
brimful with figures dancing,
a hat for trekking through snow.
Bells vibrate to the rhythm of deer,
their steaming breath that hangs like thoughts
we don't have language for,
soft and imprecise against the blue.

Instead I push you in your buggy to the bus.
We wait and watch clouds gather overhead.
You point to everything – traffic, dogs,
graffiti, all of equal moment to your eye.
And when it comes I haul the buggy up
the angled step and then stop short –
I feel his shadow falling every time.
Is this the seat he sat in on his mission,
staring out the window, maybe humming
to himself, stroking the metal toy that rests
so easy on his knee in the plastic bag?
Or is he one behind, his breath on my neck
curdling with mine? I hear the rabid humour:
Our hero, Rambo Stone. Next time you go
to Milltown take a tank. . .

I pull your cap down tight
around your ears. Let's pretend
that we are somewhere far,
you in your red-painted sleigh
me a dark-eyed doe
that has not smelt the lust of dogs
bearing you away.

ANATOMY OF AN ARTIST

*This gentleman has compiled a particular treatise of anatomy
. . . and of whatever can be reasoned about in the bodies both of
men and women, in a way that has never yet been done by any
other man.*

Antonio de Beatis, 1517

The ringed bird tilts
lopsided into the blue.
Trailing her quill
in the scientist's ink
she plots the impossible journey
of fall and spring.

Da Vinci sought a similar curve,
dissecting every sinew in the wing
to reach where skylarks sing. For every Icarus
the downward flight begins.
Only in two dimensions
under the sun

did he spread unerring wings
divining the instinct
that leans on the wind,
that transfuses everything.
He returned all the parts to the thing itself
the vessel to its dreams.

HARVEST

She sits on –
some say slow-witted, others brave
as the locust machine grows black.

Earth shuddering beneath the shell
beneath the rim of her body
threatening to crack.

Air chokes
corroding lungs
the steering hand could crush.

She sits on
in a shrinking world
that cannot hold the jarring of her note.

Chaff bales out behind, a neat-bound
box for feathers, blood, bone
and untried voice.

He lasts longer
solitary
sounding out a harsh lament

for all their flightless futures
laid in a nest
our future won't accommodate.

Bird
that will not build above the corn
casually reaped.

WAITING FOR RAIN

The shimmering volcano in the kitchen
scorches the tips of a child's tendril fingers
claiming as I did your land as my own.

The deep centre threatens to seep through the fissures
that furrow like nerves along brittle terrain.

I bear the name 'mother' carved on my heart-land
where cattle still graze as ash coats their backs.

A memory of rainfall beats in dry places
where lava is choking the lark in its path.

I open the door and imagine a cloudburst
I touch my own earth and remember the dance.

'SHE COULD NOT FIND HER NO'

Emily Dickinson

There was this boss poet
a democratically elected one
the big daddy of words
(he had a way with them)
and everyone knew who to go to
when they wanted a word said
in the right place
that would open doors.

This boss poet made poems of no words –
no way, not ever, no how
(such know-how
that I for one was struck dumb
with what might have been admiration).
Anyway, he took my breath away
with his no words
(which no one listened to
without a sense of no wonder
without an amen).

And without saying yes once
I surrendered all my no's
as the boss poet prayed
for the grass to turn blue
and grow not an inch taller.

COMMUNITY RELATION

Who is this urgent, longed-for creature
tugging the milk from my body,
who dreamed nine months in my inner sea
tumbling, kicking, hiccupping
while ceasefires were declared
in the world that she will absorb
like litmus paper?

Who can tell when the cord will be cut?
Wounds heal?
When recognition will blossom in a smile?
What the first new-coined words
of a common tongue might be?

To gather a child up to your shoulder,
cheek to your cheek,
is to hazard the perilous gift of love
into a no-man's land.

ANN McKAY

THE FARMER WANTS A WIFE

The farmer wants a wife
Wants a child
Wants a nurse
Wants a dog.
The dog wants a bone.
The bone doesn't get to want,
Or the bone may want
But the bone doesn't get.
The bone is left alone.
We all clap the bone.
The bone shuts its eyes
Against the thumps
And tries to laugh
And not to care
Until the thumping stops,
And bone as farmer
Picks the underdog
That picks its bone
With malice gleeful
And aforethought
To land it in the soup
For a good stewing.

ON THE MOUNTAIN

On the mountain
Stands a lady.
Who she is
I do not know.
All she wants is
Gold and silver.
So come in my someone-oh.
The callers' noose about the neck
To lead aside
For a whispered special offer.
Would you like a silver dolls' house?
Or a gold tea-set?
Well, do you know what,
Lady of the mountain?
Better than all
Your gold and silver stuff
Are the arms of the friends
About my neck
And the hot hiss of the secret
In both ears at once.

BLACKBIRDS NESTING

Do not disturb them.
Do not part the leaves.
Do not look her in the eye
Where she sits, unable to move.
Do not alarm her partner
Who does lookout with voluble fluster,
Marks out the space
Like a shooting range
Where she sits fixed
With what she is making
About her legs,
Between her bones,
Among her feathers,
Blood warm.
Do not look
Or touch, they say.
But you do.
Why do you?
Just.
You just do.
Because the one's call draws you
Like a telephone shrilling,
And the other's glinting eye pulls yours
Like a key in a door
That you must and must not open.
And so you do (look and touch),
Spring after barren spring
Until one year
When you don't
And something, like a clutch of baldy scaldies,
   hatches out.

DEAR GHOST

Dear ghost,
your haunts are harder
to discern these days: the betokening
foreground of Foyle College for
Boys; the Mourne Bar, second floor, in thick
of tobacco smoke and banter; back of the APCK,
Shipquay Street, in company
with Camus, Hesse,
Kierkegaard . . .

Edgy now in border
seaboard town you won't stay
still, in these unsettled
settings, long enough for me to re-
embody
you the way your memory fills my
present form with feeling.

Dear ghost, your passing makes
of oily puddles rainbows
for an instant, living streams out of
the tonnage of incessant
rain; you make
well-tended shrines
of all the places where our faces
nearly kissed, the
endless possibilities
enshrined
of whatever it was that
never was
never was
between us.

Dear ghost,
years pass, shift
leaves, the names of places,
bricks, mortar, mud, faces
troubled like clouds.

On Friday nights
at eight, off Claudy bus alights
my ghost, makes after
you, dear ghost,
reads visages
of puddles, measures
the river's spiritual charge, plumbs the deep
streets' darkest cavities for human
warmth, for signs of your soft
passing.

The intention not
to press hard questions, but just,
in undisputed
air,
to stake a claim,
to map out
love
that was
and is, dear
ghost.

LAKESIDE NURSING HOME

What will you see of the lough
From the catalogue chair with no give,
But a half-hearted overseen wipe of silver –
The mirror image, shattered by a cough,
Of tarnished lining, tainted plate,
Only treasure of clouded inner eye,
That takes as little notice of the fretting fly
As of poised helicopter that pulsates,
Affecting showy metamorphosis.
You, now disregarded but for itemised attentions,
Pay no heed to outlandish nor familiar pretensions,
Vague noises at your back from the populous hills.

IRISH LACE

On your lap a cone of cotton thread
Whiter than sifted icing sugar,
Fine as filaments of feather.
You hunched and squinted, read

Old patterns of omens – shards, mackerel
Skies – as you plied the blunt hook,
To twine and loop, tug and poke –
Iceplate of oak leaves in full rain barrel.

Shadows of flame addressed the room.
Your puffed, with one indented, sponge-cake fingers
Reworked your mother's message in the spider's
Craft, made tiny all-too-perfect roses bloom.

FRIDA KAHLO'S *SELF-PORTRAIT WITH BONITO*

On my dark-clad shoulder a perky parakeet,
Beak set in fixed companionable grin.
Pretty Polly. Seed-crusher. Bonito.
My formal-black constrainèd hair is festive,
My confluent brows a cornfield crow in joyous flight,
My downturned mouth a ripe red brimming purse.
Through the dark glass of each brown iris
The light of the projector shines
Illuminating what my heart has seen.

I have in mind a vigorous tree,
Leaves multiplying sunward,
Where I, a short-term resident,
Go openly about my business –
Incision, fretwork, mastication
Of the living host –
Her forest of veins,
Her plains of skin,
The mountain ranges of her innards.
All I do, and for one reason only,
The working of a hammock for discreet repose,
In which to dream a new self,
Buoy up the hefty hungry body
On leaded wings of stained-glass fancy.

Here I float, there I dangle –
A nectar-sipping, blossom-kissing
Section of intestine that
My heart has seen.

My heart has seen
My heaven blue, myself and fellow grubs,
My Eden gnawed,
And I, transcendent hovering dithering moth,
Antennae, wings and abdomen
Confounding easy ecstasy.
No ready falsifying picture
Of my Tree of Life
Without us parasites.

I paint my friend Bonito's feathers
With a steady bristle touch,
My brush a branch of tight-bound offshoots –
Plucked filaments of my moustache.

BIOGRAPHICAL NOTES

RUTH CARR, born in 1953, was brought up in Belfast, where she is now raising a family of her own and teaching part-time. Her poems have been published in various journals and anthologies, including *Map-makers' Colours* (Nu-Age Editions, 1988), *Sleeping with Monsters* (Wolfhound Press, 1990) and *Ireland's Women* (Gill and Macmillan, 1994). She edited an anthology of Northern Irish women writers, *The Female Line* (Northern Ireland Women's Rights Movement, 1985) and is currently associate editor of *HU* (*Honest Ulsterman*).

MARGARET CURRAN was born in Belfast, where she lives with her husband and daughter. She has had poems published in the *Kilkenny Literary Review*, the *Midland Review* (USA), *Ogham* and in the local press.

ELAINE GASTON was born in 1960, and raised in the townland of Carrowreagh, County Antrim. She is currently living and working in Belfast. She has been published in anthologies and journals, including *HU* (*Honest Ulsterman*), *Peterloo Poets 6*, *Poetry Ireland Review*, and *Verse*.

PIA GORE was born in 1961 and grew up in Cushendall, Country Antrim. She is currently living in Bangor, County Down. She is an artist who has exhibited in England and Ireland. Her poems have been published in *Encounter*, *Fortnight*, *Horizon* and other magazines and newspapers.

ANN McKAY was born in 1955 in Dungannon, County Tyrone, and lived from the age of five in Drumahoe outside Londonderry. She studied in Dublin, has taught in east Belfast, England and Zimbabwe, and now lives and works in Omagh, County Tyrone. Her stories and poems have appeared in the

Stony Thursday Book, North and *The Wall-Reader* (Arlen House, 1979). She co-edited *Our Say*, a book of Derry women's writing, in 1992. She teaches creative writing.

EILISH MARTIN was born in 1945 and brought up in Belfast, where she lives with her husband and children. She returned to writing poetry in 1992, and since then has been published in the *Sunday Tribune*'s 'New Irish Writing', was shortlisted for the Hennessy Literary Award, and was a prizewinner in the 1995 National Women's Poetry Competition (and published in *Women's Work*, The Works, Wexford).

JOAN NEWMANN was born in County Armagh in 1942. She was a member of the Philip Hobsbaum Belfast Writers' Group. A collection of her poetry, *Coming of Age*, was published by Blackstaff Press in 1995. She teaches creative writing, and lives in Ballycastle, County Antrim.

KATE NEWMANN was born in County Down in 1965. She is the compiler of the *Dictionary of Ulster Biography* (Institute of Irish Studies, 1994), won the James Prize in 1988 for an extract of her Cretan journal 'Siga, Siga', and in 1996 was a prizewinner in PHRAS. She lives in Ballycastle, County Antrim.

GRÁINNE TOBIN was born in Armagh in 1951 and now lives in Newcastle, County Down. She has two children, and teaches in Shimna Integrated College in Newcastle. She has had poems published in *Cyphers*, *Fortnight*, and *HU* (*Honest Ulsterman*), and in Dolly Mixtures anthologies.

MARY TWOMEY was born in 1938 in Downpatrick, County Down, where she still lives and works part-time as a teacher. She has written sporadically for about ten years, and was published in *The Female Line* (Northern Ireland Women's Rights Movement, 1985).

SALLY WHEELER was born in 1937 in England and has lived in Belfast since 1968. She is a member of various writing groups and also writes short fiction, and paints. Her poems have been published in the *Women's Work* anthologies, and in the *Cúirt Journal*.

ANN ZELL was born in the USA in 1933 and raised in Idaho. She came to Belfast in 1980 and began writing seriously in 1986. She has been published in a number of Irish journals, and in *Verse*, the *Atlanta Review*, and *Virago New Poets* (1993).

30630

SCOTTISH POETRY LIBRARY
5 Crichton's Close
Edinburgh EH8 8DT
Tel: 0131 557 2876

AA9 0029819 5B

JF/D.

This book is due for return on or before the last date shown below.

1 8 FEB 2004

2 6 APR 2006

1 3 OCT 2010

WITHDRAWN FROM STOCK
MARKED BY STAFF AT THIS DATE

Don Gresswell Ltd., London, N.21, Cat. No. 1208

Stories linking with the History
National Curriculum Key Stage 2.

To the child migrants, their children
and grandchildren.

First published in 1999 by Franklin Watts
96 Leonard Street, London EC2A 4XD

Text © Malachy Doyle 1999

The right of to be identified as the Author of this
Work has been asserted by him in accordance with
the Copyright, Designs and Patents Act, 1988

Editor: Sarah Snashall
Designer: Jason Anscomb
Consultant: Dr Anne Millard, BA Hons, Dip Ed, Phd

A CIP catalogue record for this book
is available from the British Library.

ISBN   0 7496 3370 0 (hbk)
ISBN 0 7496 3542 8 (pbk)

Dewey Classification 941.084

Printed in Great Britain